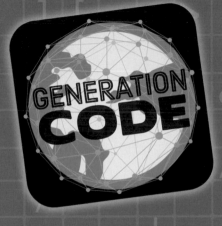

GENERATION CODE

I'M A JAVASCRIPT GAMES MAKER:
THE BASICS

Max Wainewright

WAYLAND
www.waylandbooks.co.uk

CONTENTS

INTRODUCTION

Learn how to code your own fun games using JavaScript. JavaScript is a language originally used to make web pages more interactive. It is now used to create online games that will run on both computers and mobile devices. Enjoy creating the simple projects in this book and you will be on your way to becoming a JavaScript expert!

TIPS TO REDUCE BUGS

⇨ If you are making your own web page, spend time drawing a diagram and planning it before you start. Try changing values if things don't work, and don't be afraid to start again – you will learn from it.

⇨ Practise debugging! Make a very simple web page and get a friend to change one line of code while you're not looking. Can you fix it?

⇨ When things are working properly, stop and look through your code so you understand each line. Experiment and change your code, and try out different values. To be good at debugging, you need to understand what each line of your code does and how it works.

You could use a plain text editor to create your code.

mygame.html

```
<script>
alert('Press any key to start')
</script>
```

This will work fine but can be quite fiddly, as the software won't give you any help.

The best thing to use for the activities in this book is an offline HTML editor. This will support you as you type your code, but also give you the opportunity to learn the JavaScript code.

There are two separate windows that you'll be using:

Sublime Text

```
<script>
  var score=0;
  var seconds=0;
  function moveIt(){
    score++;
```

The **text editor** to enter your JavaScript code.

Web Browser

SCORE: 7

The **browser** to view the program.

There are many different browsers you can use. We recommend using Google Chrome for the activities in this book. Make sure you have the latest version installed on your computer before you start.

You will also learn some HTML, as well as JavaScript, in this book. HTML is the language used to build web pages. JavaScript is the language that brings those pages to life!

GETTING STARTED

You need a text editor to start coding in JavaScript. There will probably be a simple text editor already on your computer, called Notepad (if you have Windows) or TextEdit (on a Mac). This will be sufficient for you to get started, but it will be much easier to create JavaScript if you download a more powerful text editor. In this book, we will use a text editor called Sublime Text. There are many others you could download, such as Brackets or Notepad++ — all of these are free for you to try out.

STEP I – FIND THE SUBLIME TEXT WEBSITE

⇨ Open your web browser and visit **www.sublimetext.com**

www.sublimetext.com

STEP 2 – START DOWNLOADING

⇨ Click the **Download** button near the top of the web page.

⇨ Choose which version of Sublime Text you need. If you are not sure, then ask an adult to help you find the correct version: click the Apple menu, then **About** if you are using a Mac. On a PC click the **Start** menu, select **System**, and click **About**.

Download

- OSX (10.7 or later is required)
- Windows
- Windows 64 bit

STEP 3 – INSTALL THE SOFTWARE

⇨ Some web browsers will then ask you to run the installation program. Choose **Run**.

⇨ If this does not happen, don't panic. The installer file should have been downloaded to your computer. Look in your **Downloads** folder for it. Double-click it to start installing your new text editor. You should get a big white or grey box giving you instructions on what to do next. Follow these instructions to complete the installation.

STEP 4 – RUNNING SUBLIME TEXT

On a PC:

⇨ Click **Start > Programs > Sublime Text**. Or just click **Sublime Text** if it appears in the **Recently added** section.

On a Mac:

⇨ Click **Finder**.

⇨ Click **Applications**.

Applications

⇨ Make a shortcut by dragging **Sublime Text** from **Finder** on to your dock at the bottom of the **Desktop**.

⇨ Click the **Sublime Text** icon.

STEP 5 – SAY HELLO

⇨ Carefully type this into lines 1, 2 and 3 of your text editor.

Sublime Text

```
1  <script>
2      alert("Hello")
3  </script>
```

Mark the start of a JavaScript section.

Show a message box saying 'Hello'. The code will automatically indent.

Mark the end of the JavaScript section.

STEP 6 – SAVE YOUR CODE

⇨ Click **File > Save**.

⇨ Save to your **Documents** folder.

⇨ Type **hello.html** as the filename.

STEP 7 – VIEW YOUR PAGE

⇨ Open your **Documents** folder.

⇨ Find the **hello.html** file and double-click it.

⇨ Your web page should now load in your normal web browser.

⇨ You should get a message saying 'Hello'.

Documents/hello.html

Hello

OK

WHY USE JAVASCRIPT INSIDE HTML CODE?

Although we are coding with JavaScript, we need to put our file inside some HTML code to make it work. HTML stands for HyperText Markup Language and is the language used to build web pages.

HTML is used to describe what objects, or elements, are shown on a web page. If you are creating a simple game, you need to use HTML to add an image and some text to show the score. However, HTML can't make the image move or the score change.

JavaScript is added to tell the image to move around when different keys are pressed, or the mouse is clicked. It can also be used to display the score and make it change. We need to use both HTML and JavaScript to make a more interesting game. JavaScript was designed to be added to HTML pages to make them more interactive.

You will learn about using different elements of HTML with JavaScript as you work through the projects in this book.

MATHS QUIZ

Now let's code a simple maths quiz. This will be a chance for you to get to know JavaScript a bit better. If you've done some coding before, you will be familiar with the idea of variables and IF statements. We will look at how to use these concepts in JavaScript.

> The syntax is really important in JavaScript. Syntax means making sure all the commands and symbols are typed correctly.

STEP 1 – START YOUR TEXT EDITOR

On a PC:

⇨ Click **Start > Programs > Sublime Text.**

On a Mac:

⇨ Click the Sublime Text icon (see page 5 for help).

STEP 2 – ENTER THE CODE

⇨ Carefully type in your maths quiz questions. For the question 'What is 8 x 8?' (Answer: 64), add the following code into your text editor for lines 1 to 6:

Sublime Text

```
1  <script>
2      answer=prompt("What is 8 x 8?");
3      if(answer==64){
4          alert("Correct!");
5      }
6  </script>
```

Start the script.

Ask a question.

If the answer is 64, then:

Show a message box saying 'Correct!'.

End the script.

In JavaScript, the amount you indent your code won't affect how it works. However, it will make it easier to read. Your text editor may also do this automatically.

Just as you end a sentence with a full stop, you should end JavaScript statements with a semi-colon(;).

STEP 3 – SAVE YOUR CODE

⇨ Click **File > Save** and type **quiz.html** as the filename.

⇨ Make sure you save it in your **Documents** folder.

STEP 4 – VIEW YOUR WORK

⇨ Open your **Documents** folder and double-click the **quiz.html** file. Your program should run in your web browser.

⇨ Test your page by answering correctly, then reloading your page and giving the wrong answer.

Documents/quiz.html

What is 8 x 8?

Cancel   OK

Reload

STEP 5 – RANDOMISE!

⇨ Change your code, in the following way, so random numbers are picked for the question:

Make a variable called a.

Create a random number between 0 and 1.

```
var a=Math.round(Math.random()*10);
```

Round to the nearest whole number.

Multiply it by 10.

Sublime Text

```
1  <script>
2      var a=Math.round(Math.random()*10);
3      var b=Math.round(Math.random()*10);
4      answer=prompt("what is "+a+" x "+b+"?");
5      if(answer==a*b){
6          alert("Correct!")
7      }
8  </script>
```

Use the + sign to join the string 'what is' to the value stored in the variable **a**.

Check to see if the answer entered is the same as **a** multiplied by (*) **b**.

STEP 6 – SAVE AND REFRESH

⇨ Save your new code.

⇨ Reload your browser to see the changes. Each time you reload it you should get a new random question.

 ⚑ Enjoy playing your quiz!

CUSTOMISE

• Change your code so it asks harder questions, using bigger numbers.

◄ KEY CONCEPT

VARIABLES

Variables are part of a program that stores information. Variables are given a name that is used to point to a part of the computer's memory. A value is then stored in that part of the memory. In this quiz, variables are used to store the random numbers and the user's input.

IF STATEMENTS

Normally, each line of code works one after the other. An IF statement works differently. It checks if a particular condition is true before running a certain piece of code.

› RANDOM COLOURS

In this activity we will make a simple program that randomly sets the colour of the screen.

STEP 1 – PLANNING

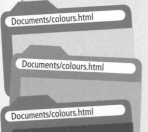

Documents/colours.html

Documents/colours.html

Documents/colours.html

⇨ Make a list of four colours to choose from.

⇨ Start a timer that changes the colour every 1000 milliseconds (which is every one second).

⇨ To change the colour:
- pick a random number from 0 to 3
- use the random number to pick one of the colours
- set the background colour to the chosen colour.

⇨ Make a special section of code called a function that will follow the steps above to change the colour. By giving the function a name – **changeColour()** – you will create a new command that will carry out the steps whenever **changeColour()** is typed.

STEP 2 – START A NEW HTML FILE

⇨ Start your text editor, or click **File** > **New**.

BRACKETS!
Square brackets are used in JavaScript to show the start and end of a list. Coders call this sort of list an array. If the array contains string (words or symbols), each one needs double quote marks around it. Curly brackets are used to show the start and end of a function.

STEP 3 – ENTER THIS CODE

⇨ Type this code in very carefully, using exactly the same spelling, symbols and upper case letters. Remember to use the US spelling of colour (color) within a JavaScript style command, but the UK spelling of colour for the name of functions (such as, **changeColour**) or variables.

Sublime Text

```
1  <script>
2    colors=["red","green","blue","yellow"];
3    var timer=window.setInterval(changeColour, 1000);
4    function changeColour(){
5      var n=Math.round(Math.random()*4);
6      document.body.style.backgroundColor=colors[n];
7    }
8  </script>
```

Start the script.

Make the list of colours.

Create a timer that will run the changeColour function every second.

Define the changeColour function.

Create a variable called **n** and give it a random value from 0 to 3.

Set the background colour.

End the function.

End the script.

STEP 4 – SAVE YOUR CODE

⇨ Click **File > Save** and type **colours.html** as the filename. Make sure you save it in your **Documents** folder.

STEP 5 – VIEW YOUR WORK

⇨ Open your **Documents** folder. Double-click the **colours.html** file. Your program should run in your web browser. The screen should change colour every second.

Documents/colours.html

STEP 6 – ARRANGE YOUR SCREEN

As you start to develop more complex programs, you will need to see your code and the browser at the same time. Many programmers set up their screen so their code is on the left-hand side and their web page is shown on the right.

⇨ Resize your text editor and browser windows so your screen looks like this:

```
Sublime Text
<script>
    colors=["red","green","blue","yellow"];
    var timer=window.setInterval(changeColour, 1000);
    function changeColour(){
        var n=Math.round(Math.random()*4);
        document.body.style.backgroundColor=colors[n];
    }
</script>
```

After you have made a change to your code in the text editor, save your file.

↻ To see the effects of your changes, you need to reload the file, by clicking the **Reload this page** icon.

Documents/colours.html

CUSTOMISE

• Add more colours to the list. Make sure you put double quotation marks around each colour word and separate them with a comma.

• To pick an item from your new list, you will need to change the random number chosen. Edit the number at the end of line 5 to match the length of the list.

• Change how often a new colour is chosen by editing the end of line 3 (choosing a very low value will result in flashing colours).

KEY CONCEPT

ARRAY

An array is a list of items stored as some data. Lists are similar to variables but they can store multiple items of information. In our program, line 2 contains a list of colours.

FUNCTION

A function is a section of code combining a number of commands. The name of the function becomes a new command that runs the whole section. Lines 4 to 7 contain the function definition.

❯ ON THE MOVE

To start coding our own games we need to use some new techniques. Firstly we need to add images to the screen. We also need to be able to position the images in particular places and then make the images move. To make all this work we will use some HTML code, as well as the JavaScript.

STEP 1 – FIND A PICTURE ▶

First of all, you need to find an image to use. It needs to be placed in the same folder as your HTML file.

⇨ Go online and search for some clipart to use (see page 31).

⇨ Right-click on your chosen image. We will use a ghost image.

⇨ Click **Save Image As...**

⇨ Navigate to your **Documents** folder then click **Save**.

STEP 2 – CHECK! ▶

⇨ Open your **Documents** folder and check the picture file is there. Depending on your browser and the image it may be called **ghost.png** or **download.png**. If it is not there, go back to step 1 and try again, making sure you select the **Documents** folder.

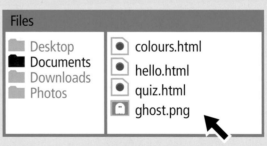

⇨ Find your image and remember its exact filename.

STEP 3 – START A NEW FILE ▶

⇨ Carefully type this code into your text editor. We are going to use some HTML code to set the background colour using the **<body>** tag. We will add an image, using the **<img>** tag.

Sublime Text

```
1  <html>
2    <body style="background-color:darkblue">
3      <img id="ghost" style="position:absolute;" src="ghost.png">
4    </body>
5  </html>
```

1 Start the HTML.
2 Set the background colour using the body tag.
3 Use the filename for the image from step 3.
4 End the body tag.
5 End the HTML.

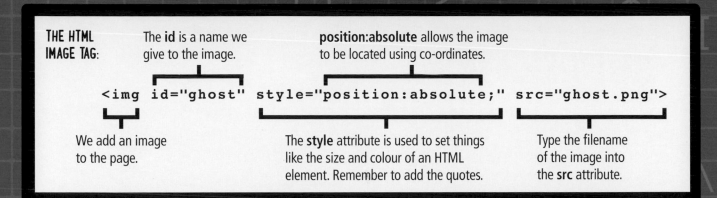

THE HTML IMAGE TAG:

The **id** is a name we give to the image.

position:absolute allows the image to be located using co-ordinates.

```
<img id="ghost" style="position:absolute;" src="ghost.png">
```

We add an image to the page.

The **style** attribute is used to set things like the size and colour of an HTML element. Remember to add the quotes.

Type the filename of the image into the **src** attribute.

STEP 4 – SAVE YOUR FILE ▷

⇨ Click **File** > **Save** and type **ghost.html** as the filename. Make sure you save it in your **Documents** folder.

STEP 5 – VIEW YOUR PAGE ▷

⇨ Open your **Documents** folder. Double-click the file and you should see it appear in your web page.

Documents/colours.html

STEP 6 – MAKE IT MOVE! ▷

⇨ We can use the timer technique from the colour-changing program to make the image move. Instead of changing the screen colour, we will change the position of the ghost every second.

⇨ Add to your original code by inserting a **<script>** section at line 5.

Sublime Text

```
1   <html>
2     <body style="background-color:darkblue">
3       <img id="ghost" style="position:absolute;" src="ghost.png">
4     </body>
5     <script>
6      var timer=window.setInterval(moveGhost, 1000);
7      function moveGhost(){
8        document.getElementById("ghost").style.left=Math.random()*900+"px";
9        document.getElementById("ghost").style.top=Math.random()*600+"px";
10     }
11    </script>
12  </html>
```

Start the JavaScript section.

Create a timer that runs the moveGhost function every 1000 milliseconds.

Define the moveGhost function.

Move the ghost to a new random position by setting its left and top style properties.

End the moveGhost function.

End JavaScript.

◄ **KEY CONCEPT**

CO-ORDINATES

Move elements, such as images, by setting their left and top style properties, or co-ordinates. Add **px** on the end of the value to measure in pixels. The co-ordinates (0,0) will always be in the top left of the browser. The maximum co-ordinates will depend on the size of the browser window.

TAGS

In HTML, all elements have an opening tag. Tags always start with **<** and end with **>**.

ATTRIBUTES

Attributes provide extra information about an HTML element, such as its size and colour.

›GET CLICKING

All computer games need the player to interact with the computer or device. To do this we need to use mouse and keyboard events. These are special bits of code that 'listen' to the mouse or keyboard and wait for certain things to happen, before running some other code.

EVENTS

We can use the **onclick** event to make some code run when an image is clicked.

The event that the program is listening for.

```
<img id="ghost" onclick="hideMe()" src="ghost.png">
```

The name of the function to run when the event takes place.

As well as the **onclick** event there are lots of other events including:

onmousedown ⇨ triggered the moment the mouse button is pressed down.

onmousemove ⇨ triggered every time the mouse is moved over an element.

onmouseup ⇨ triggered the moment the mouse button is released.

onkeydown ⇨ triggered when keys on the keyboard are pressed.

STEP 1 – START A NEW FILE ▶

⇨ Carefully add this code into your text editor.

Sublime Text

```
1  <html>
2    <img id="ghost" onclick="hideMe()" src="ghost.png">
3    <script>
4      function hideMe(){
5        document.getElementById("ghost").style.display="none";
6      }
7    </script>
8  </html>
```

Use the ghost picture from page 10. When it is clicked, run the function called **hideMe**.

Use the filename for the image from page 10.

Define the function called hideMe.

Hide the ghost when the function is run.

End the function.

STEP 2 – SAVE AND VIEW YOUR FILE

⇨ Click **File** > **Save** and type **events.html** as the filename.

⇨ Make sure you save it in your **Documents** folder.

⇨ Open your **Documents** folder. Double-click the **events.html** file. You should see your image.

Documents/events.html

⇨ Click the image to make it disappear.

HIDING HTML ELEMENTS

Set the **style.display** property of an element to **none** to make it disappear. Set it to **block** to make it appear again.

Select the element to hide (the ghost), by using its ID (its name).

The value you are giving to the property.

```
document.getElementById("ghost").style.display="none";
```

The property you want to change.

STEP 3 – RUNAWAY!

We are going to use the **onmouseenter** event in the next example. This is triggered just as the mouse is moved over an element. It doesn't wait for the mouse to be pressed. When you move the mouse over the ghost, it will jump to a new random position.

⇨ Edit your code from page 12.

Remember to set **position:absolute**.

Sublime Text

```
1  <html>
2    <img id="ghost" style="position:absolute;" onmouseenter="runAway()
   src="ghost.png">
3    <script>
4      function runAway(){
5        document.getElementById("ghost").style.left=Math.random()*900+"px";
6        document.getElementById("ghost").style.top=Math.random()*600+"px";
7      }
8    </script>
9  </html>
```

As soon as someone tries to move the mouse over the ghost it will run the function called runAway.

Define the function called runAway.

Move the ghost to a new random position by setting its left and top style properties.

End the function.

> **Elements are the items that make up a web page, such as images. HTML uses tags to identify elements. ‹img› is the start of an image tag.**

STEP 4 – SAVE AND RELOAD

⇨ Save your code and then reload your browser to see the changes.

⇨ Try to move your mouse over the ghost. Every time your mouse moves over it, it should move away to a new position.

Documents/events.html

〉 OCTOPUS CATCHER

In this game, the player will have to catch Otto the octopus as many times as possible within 30 seconds. A timer will make Otto move every second. An **onmousedown** event will be used to check when Otto is clicked. Variables will be used to store the score and time left. The complete code for the game is listed on page 17.

STEP 1 – PLANNING ▶

The score is shown in an HTML paragraph element.

A timer will make Otto move every second. →

An **onmousedown** event is used to check when Otto is caught. (**onmousedown** will trigger before the **onclick** event.)

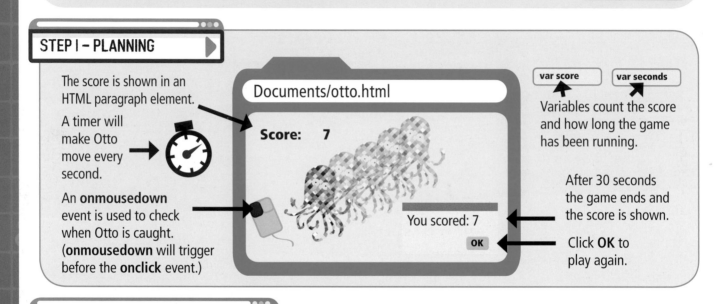

Documents/otto.html

Score: 7

You scored: 7

OK

var score   **var seconds**

Variables count the score and how long the game has been running.

After 30 seconds the game ends and the score is shown.

Click **OK** to play again.

STEP 2 – FIND A PICTURE ▶

⇨ Find an image of an octopus to use. It needs to be saved into the same folder as your HTML file.

⇨ Search for some clipart.

⇨ Right-click one image.

⇨ Click **Save Image As...**

⇨ Navigate to your **Documents** folder then click **Save**.

THE HTML PARAGRAPH TAG

Set the **style.display** property of an element to **none** to make it disappear. Set it to **block** to make it appear again.

The ID is a name we give to the paragraph.

This is called the closing tag – the end of the paragraph.

```
<p id="scoreText">Score: 0</p>
```

We are adding a paragraph to the page.

The text we want shown in the paragraph element is typed here: between the opening <p> tag and the closing </p> tag.

If we want to change the colour of the paragraph we can add a style attribute the way that we have done with the body element, and set its colour property.

⇨ Start by typing in the HTML for the game, setting out the body, image and a paragraph for the score.

```
Sublime Text
1  <html>
2  <body style="background-color:cyan">
3    <img id="otto" style="position:absolute; -webkit-
   transition: all 0.5s;" src="octopus.png" width="100"
   onmousedown="caughtIt()">
4    <p id="scoreText">Score: 0</p>
5  </body>
```

Set the background colour.

Add the image from page 12. Make sure the src property matches the name of the downloaded file.

Use a paragraph to show the score.

◄ KEY CONCEPT

TRANSITION PROPERTIES

The ghost on page 10 moved arround in quite a jerky manner. We want this game to be a bit smoother. To make this happen we will add a transition property. This means when any of Otto's properties are altered they will change gradually over a specific amount of time, instead of changing instantly. Here is the new style property used in line 3:

-webkit-transition is a property that is used to switch on gradual changes.

All of the style properties will change gradually.

```
-webkit-transition: all 0.5s;
```

The changes will be spread over 0.5s (half a second).

⇨ Click **File > Save** and type **otto.html** as the filename.

⇨ Make sure you save it in your **Documents** folder. Keep saving it every time you add a new piece of code.

⇨ We need to create our variables and start a timer. Add this code:

```
6  <script>
7    var score=0;
8    var seconds=0;
9    var timer=window.setInterval(moveIt, 1000);
```

Start the script section.

Set the score variable to 0.

Set the seconds variable to 0.

Add the timer, which will run a function called moveIt every second. Although we 'declare' it as a variable it is more like a clock. Giving it a name will mean we can stop it later.

STEP 6 – MOVE IT!

⇨ Next we need to type in the function that moves Otto.
This is similar to the **moveGhost** function on page 11.

Line	Code	Description
10	`function moveIt(){`	Define the function.
11	`seconds++;`	Count the seconds.
12	`document.getElementById("otto").style.left=Math.random()*900+"px";`	Move Otto to a new random position.
13	`document.getElementById("otto").style.top=Math.random()*700+"px";`	
14	`if(seconds>30){`	If the time limit is up:
15	`clearInterval(timer);`	Stop the timer.
16	`alert("You scored:" + score);`	Display a message box showing the score.
17	`location.reload();`	After OK is pressed, reload the page to start a new game.
18	`}`	End the block of code covered by the IF statement.
19	`}`	End the function.

STEP 7 – CAUGHT IT!

⇨ Now add the function **caughtIt**, which is run (or 'called') when Otto is clicked.

Line	Code	Description
20	`function caughtIt(){`	Define the function.
21	`score++;`	Increase the score by 1.
22	`document.getElementById("scoreText").innerText="Score: "+score;`	Change the score text. This is done by setting the innerText property.
23	`}`	
24	`</script>`	End the script.
25	`</html>`	End the HTML file.

Save your code, reload your browser, then play the game!

CUSTOMISE

• Change how long the game lasts.

• Move Otto around more quickly by altering the **-webkit-transition** value.

• Use a different image file and change the background colour to completely change the look of the game.

THE COMPLETE CODE

```
1    <html>
2    <body style="background-color:cyan">
3        <img id="otto" style="position:absolute; -webkit-transition:
         all 0.5s;"  src="octopus.png" width="100" onmousedown="caughtIt()">
4        <p id="scoreText">Score: 0</p>
5    </body>
6    <script>
7      var score=0;
8      var seconds=0;
9      var timer=window.setInterval(moveIt, 1000);
10     function moveIt(){
11       seconds++;
12       document.getElementById("otto").style.left=Math.random()*900+"px";
13       document.getElementById("otto").style.top=Math.random()*700+"px";
14       if(seconds>30){
15         clearInterval(timer);
16         alert("You scored:" + score);
17         location.reload();
18       }
19     }
20     function caughtIt(){
21       score++;
22       document.getElementById("scoreText").innerText="Score: "+score;
23     }
24   </script>
25   </html>
```

⟩ BALLOON POPPER

This game will be built with functions and the use of co-ordinates. This will make it easier for you to understand which lines of code control which parts of the game. It should help you to customise the game or reuse the functions in your own games. The animation in this game will be controlled by a much faster timer, making small changes to a balloon's location. The complete code for the game is listed on page 23.

STEP I – PLANNING

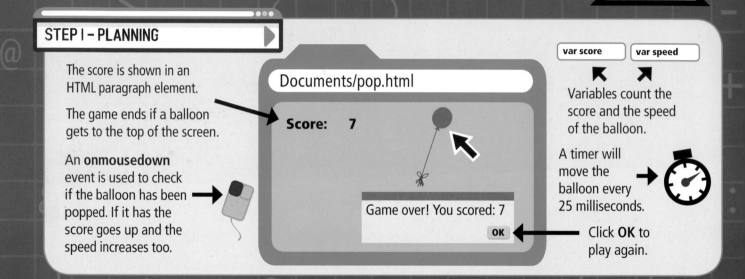

The score is shown in an HTML paragraph element.

The game ends if a balloon gets to the top of the screen.

An **onmousedown** event is used to check if the balloon has been popped. If it has the score goes up and the speed increases too.

Documents/pop.html

Score: 7

Game over! You scored: 7

OK

var score   var speed

Variables count the score and the speed of the balloon.

A timer will move the balloon every 25 milliseconds.

Click **OK** to play again.

STEP 2 – FIND A PICTURE

⇨ First of all, you need to find a balloon image to use. It needs to be placed in the same folder as your HTML file.

⇨ Go online and search for a suitable image.

⇨ Right-click one image.

⇨ Click **Save Image As...**

⇨ Navigate to your **Documents** folder then click **Save**.

STYLING A PARAGRAPH

A paragraph can be styled or formatted in a similar way to the HTML body and image elements.

color sets the colour of the text. Note the US spelling.

Separate with semi-colons.

This sets the font name of the text. If you are setting a font with spaces in its name, put quotes around the font name.

```
<p style="color:yellow; font-size:20px; font-family:Arial;">Score: 0</p>
```

The style attribute – remember the quotes.

Add **px** to set the size of the text in pixels.

The rest of the paragraph element.

16 MILLION COLOURS

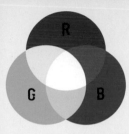

There are over 100 words that can be used to set colours. There is another more precise way to set colours, using a method that mixes together red, green and blue light. A number is given between 0 and 255 for the amount of red, green and blue in the colour, giving over 16 million combinations. This is called the RGB colour system.

The code to show bright red is 255,0,0. The red value is 255, green is 0 and blue is 0. The RGB value is then converted into a special code, called **hexadecimal**, which uses the letters A to F instead of 10 to 15. The hexadecimal code for red is written **#FF0000**.

Don't worry if you don't understand all that yet, just try using these colour codes and experiment!

Colour	Red	Green	Blue	Hex code
Red	255	0	0	FF0000
Green	0	255	0	00FF00
Blue	0	0	255	0000FF
Yellow	255	255	0	FFFF00
Purple	128	0	128	800080
White	255	255	255	FFFFFF
Black	0	0	0	000000
Dark Red	204	0	0	CC0000

> RGB codes must start with a hashtag (#) symbol. They can be capital or lower case.

STEP 3 – START A NEW FILE

⇨ Start by typing in the HTML for the game, setting out the body, image and a paragraph for the score.

Sublime Text

```
1  <html>
2  <body style="background-color:#32CD32">
3      <img id="balloon" onmousedown="popped()" src="purple-
   balloon.png" style="position:absolute; width:100px; top:500px;
   left:500px;">
4      <p id="scoreText" style="color:yellow; font-size:20px;
   font-family:Arial">Score: 0</p>
5  </body>
```

Set the background colour.

Add the image of the balloon. The src property must match the name of the downloaded file.

Add the paragraph to show the score.

STEP 4 – SAVE AND PREVIEW

⇨ Click **File** and **Save**. Type **pop.html** as the filename.

⇨ Open your **Documents** folder. Find the **pop.html** file and double-click it. The file should now load in your browser.

Documents/pop.html

Score: 7

⇨ Now we have defined the elements that go on the page, we need to start the JavaScript. At the start of this game we need to:

- create the variables we need
- define some functions to get and set co-ordinates
- define a simple function to generate random numbers
- start a timer.

6	`<script>`	Start the script section.
7	`var score=0, speed=1;`	Create variables to store the score and balloon speed.
8	`function setLeft(id,x){document.getElementById(id).style.left=x+"px";}`	Define functions to set any element's co-ordinates.
9	`function setTop(id,y){document.getElementById(id).style.top=y+"px";}`	
10	`function getLeft(id){return document.getElementById(id).offsetLeft;}`	Define functions to get any element's co-ordinates.
11	`function getTop(id){return document.getElementById(id).offsetTop;}`	
12	`function randomNumber(low,high){return(Math.floor(low+Math.random()*(1+high-low)));}`	Define a function that returns a random number between two values.
13	`var gameTimer=window.setInterval(floatUp, 25);`	The timer will run a function called floatUp every 25 milliseconds (40 times a second).

JavaScript knows the function definition has ended, because of the right curly bracket }. Coders sometimes define short, simple functions like these in a single line, as we have done here.

USING THE GET, SET AND RANDOM FUNCTIONS

You could add these functions to your own games. Here are some examples to help you use them. (Note, for the **get** and **set** functions to move an element, the element would need to have its position style property set to **absolute**.)

`setLeft("balloon",200);`	Positions the balloon 200 pixels from the left of the window.
`setTop("balloon",350);`	Positions the balloon 350 pixels from the top of the window.
`getTop("balloon");`	Returns the current distance between the balloon and the top of the window.
`randomNumber(1,6);`	Returns a random number between 1 and 6.
`randomNumber(0,100);`	Returns a random number between 0 and 100.

⇨ Next, we need to type in the function that makes the balloon float upwards.

14	`function floatUp(){`	Define the function.
15	`    var y=getTop("balloon");`	Find out how far the balloon is from the top of the window, and store it in a variable called **y**.
16	`    if(y<-100){`	If the balloon has gone past the top of the screen, then **y** will be less than -100. If it has gone past the top, then:
17	`        gameOver();`	Run the function named gameOver.
18	`    }`	End the IF block of code.
19	`    setTop("balloon",y-speed);`	Move the balloon up by using the setTop function. This is done by subtracting the speed value from **y**.
20	`}`	End the function.

The game ends when the balloon gets to the top of the screen. This is checked for in line 16 by testing to see if the top of the balloon is less than -100.

Once the balloon gets beyond the top of the screen, the **getTop** function will return a negative number, - 100.

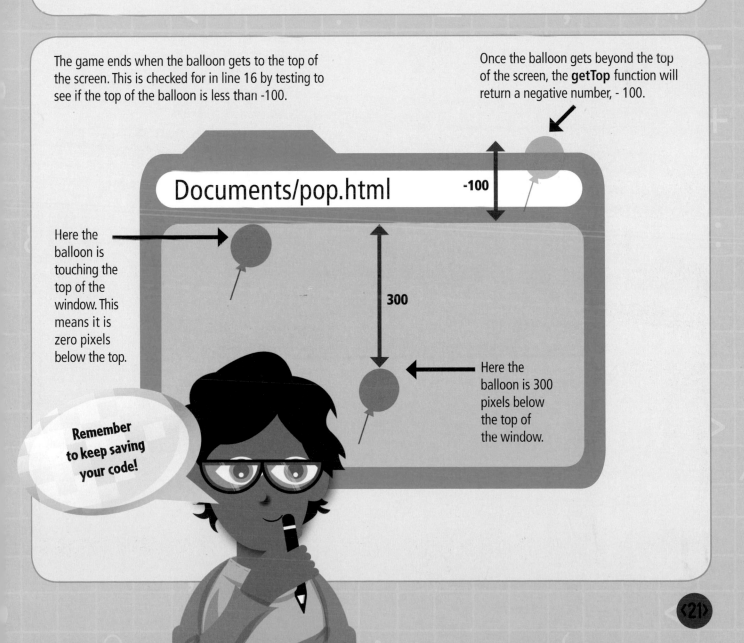

Documents/pop.html

-100

300

Here the balloon is touching the top of the window. This means it is zero pixels below the top.

Here the balloon is 300 pixels below the top of the window.

Remember to keep saving your code!

STEP 7 – POPPED

⇨ We need to make quite a few things happen when the balloon is popped (clicked). Add this function:

```
21    function popped(){
22      score++;
23      speed++;
24      document.getElementById("scoreText").innerText="Score: "+score;
25      setLeft("balloon", randomNumber(0,window.innerWidth-100));
26      setTop("balloon", window.innerHeight);
27    }
```

Define the function.

This means: make the score go up by one.

Make the next balloon move faster by increasing the speed by one.

Show the score at the top of the screen.

Set how far the balloon is from the left of the screen to be a random value.

Move the balloon to the very bottom of the screen.

STEP 8 – THE END OF THE GAME

⇨ When the balloon reaches the top of the screen, the game is over. When this happens we need to run the following code:

```
28    function gameOver(){
29      clearInterval(gameTimer);
30      alert("Game Over! You scored: "+ score);
31      location.reload();
32    }
```

Define the function.

Stop the timer running so the balloon won't move any more.

Show a message telling the player the game is over and showing their score.

This command will reload the page and make the game start again. (If you don't want this to happen, leave this line blank.)

STEP 9 – LAST LINES

⇨ Finally, add these two lines to show the end of the script section and the end of the HTML.

```
33    </script>
34    </html>
```

 Save your file, reload the browser, then play!

THE COMPLETE CODE

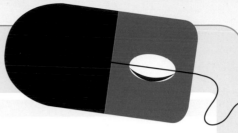

```
1    <html>
2    <body style="background-color:#32CD32">
3        <img id="balloon" onmousedown="popped()" style="position:absolute;
     width:100px; top:500px; left:500px;" src="purple-balloon.png">
4        <p id="scoreText" style="color:yellow; font-size:20px; font-family:Arial;">Score: 0</p>
5    </body>
6    <script>
7        var score=0, speed=1;
8        function setLeft(id,x){document.getElementById(id).style.left=x+"px";}
9        function setTop(id,y){document.getElementById(id).style.top=y+"px";}
10       function getLeft(id){return document.getElementById(id).offsetLeft;}
11       function getTop(id){return document.getElementById(id).offsetTop;}
12       function randomNumber(low,high){return (Math.floor(low+ Math.random()*(1+high-low)));}
13       var gameTimer=window.setInterval(floatUp, 25);
14       function floatUp(){
15           var y=getTop("balloon");
16           if(y<-100){
17               gameOver();
18           }
19           setTop("balloon",y-speed);
20       }
21       function popped(){
22           score++,
23           speed++;
24           document.getElementById("scoreText").innerText="Score: "+score;
25           setLeft("balloon", randomNumber(0,window.innerWidth-100));
26           setTop("balloon", window.innerHeight);
27       }
28       function gameOver(){
29           clearInterval(gameTimer);
30           alert("Game Over! You scored: "+ score);
31           location.reload();
32       }
33   </script>
34   </html>
```

CUSTOMISE

• Make the game harder by making the balloon smaller. Alter its width property in line 3.

• Set the speed of the balloon to a random value when it has been clicked.

• Create a different game by using a different image and different background. You could try making the object move downwards or to the right?

BONE CATCHER

In this game, the player controls a dog, moving it left and right to catch a bone as it drops down the screen. Arrow key presses make the dog move left and right. The game uses some of the same functions as the previous program to set co-ordinates and create random numbers. Both the bone and dog move at intervals of 50 pixels. The complete code for the game is listed on page 29.

STEP 1 – PLANNING

The score is shown in an HTML paragraph element.

A timer will move the bone every 200 milliseconds.

It then checks if the dog and bone co-ordinates match. If they do, this means the dog has caught the bone, making the score increase.

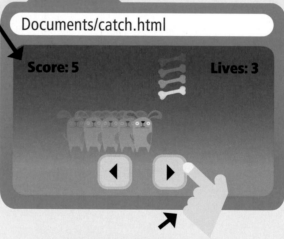

Documents/catch.html

Score: 5   Lives: 3

Pressing the left and right arrow keys will change the dog's **x** co-ordinates, and therefore the position of the dog.

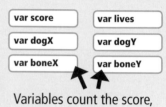

var score   var lives
var dogX   var dogY
var boneX   var boneY

Variables count the score, number of lives left, and **x** and **y** co-ordinates of the dog and of the bone.

When there are no lives left, the game ends.

Game over! You scored: 5

Click **OK** to play again.

STEP 2 – FIND AN IMAGE

Find an image of a dog and an image of a bone to use. Save them in the same folder as your HTML file.

⇨ Go online and search for a suitable image.

⇨ Right-click one image.

⇨ Click **Save Image As...**

⇨ Navigate to your **Documents** folder then click **Save**.

STEP 3 – START A NEW FILE

⇨ Start by typing in the HTML for the game, setting out the body, image and a paragraph for the score.

Sublime Text

```
1  <html>
2  <body style="background: -webkit-linear-gradient(blue, green);">
3    <img id="dog" style="position:absolute; width:50px; top:500px;
   left:300px; -webkit-transition: all 0.2s;" src="dog.png">
4    <img id="bone" style="position:absolute; width:50px;  top:0px;
   left:0px; -webkit-transition: all 0.2s;" src="bone.png">
5     <p id="scoreTB" style="position:absolute; left:50px;
   color:yellow; font-size:28px; font-family:Arial;">Score: 0</p>
6      <p id="livesTB" style="position:absolute; right:50px;
   color:yellow; font-size:28px; font-family:Arial;">Lives: 3</p>
7  </body>
```

Set the background colour.

Add the image of the dog and of the bone. In each case, the src property must match the file you downloaded.

Add a paragraph showing the score.

Show the lives remaining. Note this is set 50 pixels from the right edge.

STEP 4 – SAVE AND PREVIEW

⇨ Click **File** and **Save**. Type **catch.html** as the filename.

⇨ Open your **Documents** folder. Find the **catch.html** file and double-click it. The file should now load in your browser. The images won't move yet (as there is no code telling them to), but the page should look something like this:

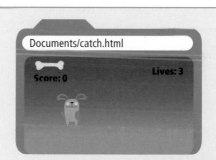

Documents/catch.html

Score: 0   Lives: 3

KEY CONCEPT

COLOUR GRADIENTS

In the games we have created so far, we have set the background to be a solid colour. However, we can create some great effects by using something called colour gradients. This means using two colours and blending them together gradually. Experiment with the following code from line 2:

Change these

```
<body style="background: -webkit-linear-gradient(blue, green);">

<body style="background: -webkit-linear-gradient(red, yellow);">
```

⇨ Now that we have defined the elements that go on the page, we need to begin the JavaScript. At the start of this game we need to:

- create the variables we need
- define some functions to get and set co-ordinates
- define a simple function to generate random numbers
- start a timer.

8	`<script>`	Start the Javascript section.
9	`var score=0, lives=3, dogX=6, dogY=10, boneX=8, boneY=0;`	Create variables to store the score, number of lives, and dog and bone co-ordinates.
10	`function setLeft(id,x){document.getElementById(id).style.left=x+"px";}`	Define functions to set any element's co-ordinates.
11	`function setTop(id,y){document.getElementById(id).style.top=y+"px";}`	
12	`function randomNumber(low,high){return(Math.floor(low+Math.random()*(1+high-low)));}`	Define a function that returns a random number between two values.
13	`var gameTimer=window.setInterval(moveBone, 200);`	Set the timer to run a function called moveBone every 200 milliseconds (5 times per second).
14	`document.onkeydown=handleKeys;`	

Run a function called handleKeys, whenever a key is pressed on the keyboard.

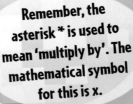

LISTENING TO THE KEYBOARD

In this game, the dog will move when the arrow keys are pressed on the keyboard. To do this, we need to set up something called an event listener, which will 'listen' to the keyboard and run some code if a key is pressed. This is similar to the **onclickmouse** event listener explained on page 12. Look at line 14:

```
document.onkeydown=handleKeys;
```

The event that the program is waiting (listening) for. Other keyboard events include **onkeyup** and **onkeypress**.

The name of the function to run when the event takes place.

Remember, the asterisk * is used to mean 'multiply by'. The mathematical symbol for this is x.

POSITIONING THE DOG AND BONE

The dog's co-ordinates are stored in **dogX** and **dogY**, and the bone's co-ordinates are in **boneX** and **boneY**.

To make sure the dog has a chance to catch the bone, we will make each of them move on an invisible grid. Each square in the grid will be 50 pixels wide and 50 pixels high. To set the left position of the dog we therefore multiply **boneX** by 50, and to set the top value we multiply **boneY** by 50.

If **dogX** is 2, and **dogY** is 3, then this is what would happen:

The dog is 2 * 50 = 100 pixels in from the left.

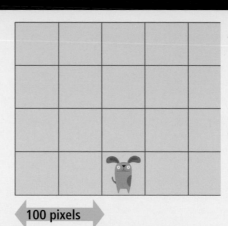

150 pixels

100 pixels

The dog is 3 * 50 = 150 pixels down from the top.

STEP 6 – PRESS ANY KEY

⇨ When a key is pressed by the player, we need to move the dog left or right. The direction moved depends on which key is pressed. We need to add a special sort of variable called a parameter to our function, which will store information about the key that has been pressed. Type **(e)** after the function name to add the parameter. Each key on the keyboard has a specific code linked to it. The left arrow has a code of 37, the right arrow's code is 39. The code for the key pressed will be stored in **e.keyCode**.

```
15    function handleKeys(e){
16        if(e.keyCode==37){dogX--;}
17        if(e.keyCode==39){dogX++;}
18        setLeft("dog", dogX*50);
19        setTop("dog", dogY*50);
20    }
```

Define a function called handleKeys. Information about the key press event will be put into the variable called **e**.

Make dogX go down by 1 (dogX-- means subtract 1 from the value in dogX), if the code for the left arrow key has been sent.

Make dogX go up by 1 (dogX++ means add 1 to dogX), if the code for the right arrow key has been passed to the function.

Set the new position for the dog.

STEP 7 – MOVE THE BONE

⇨ The bone gets moved by the timer every 200 milliseconds. Although this means it only moves 5 times a second, it will look quite smooth because we have used the **webkit-transition** property. The timer runs this function.

```
21    function moveBone(){
22        boneY=boneY+=1;
23        setLeft("bone", boneX*50);
24        setTop("bone", boneY*50);
25        if(boneY>dogY+5){missedBone();}
26        if((dogX==boneX) && (dogY==boneY)){caughtBone();}
27    }
```

Define the function.

Make the boneY variable go up by one (you could type this code as boneY++ if you want to save time!).

Set the new position for the bone. (boneX only changes if it has been caught or missed).

Run the missedBone function, if the bone has been missed and has fallen below the dog.

Run the caughtBone function, if the bone has been caught by the dog and they both have the same **x** and **y** co-ordinates.

STEP 8 – MISSED IT

⇨ If the dog hasn't caught the bone then the player loses a life. We test for this in line 25, by comparing the **y** co-ordinates of both images. If the bone is more than 5 grid squares lower down than the dog, then it has missed it. When that happens this code needs to run:

Line	Code	Description
28	`function missedBone(){`	Define the function.
29	`boneY=0;`	Move the bone to the top.
30	`boneX=randomNumber(2,16);`	Position it a random amount in from the left of the screen.
31	`lives--;`	Lose a life.
32	`document.getElementById("livesTB").innerText="Lives: "+lives;`	Display how many lives are left.
33	`if(lives==0){gameOver();}`	Run the gameOver function, if there are no lives left.
34	`}`	

STEP 9 – CAUGHT IT

⇨ The code in line 26 checks to see if the bone and dog co-ordinates are equal. If they match, the following function runs:

Line	Code	Description
35	`function caughtBone(){`	Define the function.
36	`boneY=0;`	Move the bone to the top.
37	`boneX=randomNumber(2,16);`	Position the bone a random amount in from the left of the screen.
38	`score++;`	Increase the score by 1.
39	`document.getElementById("scoreTB").innerText="Score: "+score;`	Show the score.
40	`}`	

STEP 10 – THE END

⇨ If the dog doesn't catch the bone and there are no lives left, the game is over. Type in this function:

Line	Code	Description
41	`function gameOver(){`	Define the function.
42	`alert("Game Over! You scored: "+ score);`	Show a message telling the player the game is over and showing their score.
43	`location.reload();`	Reload the page and make the game start again.
44	`}`	

STEP 11 – CLOSING TAGS

Finally, type in a closing script tag and a closing HTML tag to end the file.

Line	Code
45	`</script>`
46	`</html>`

Save your file, reload the browser and enjoy your game!

THE COMPLETE CODE

```
1   <html>
2   <body style="background: -webkit-linear-gradient(blue, green);">
3       <img id="dog" style="position:absolute; width:50px; top:500px; left:300px;
    -webkit-transition: all 0.2s;"src="dog.png">
4       <img id="bone" style="position:absolute; width:50px; top:0px; left:0px;
    -webkit-transition: all 0.2s;" src="bone.png">
5       <p id="scoreTB" style="position:absolute; left:50px; color:yellow;
    font-size:28px; font-family:Arial;">Score: 0</p>
6       <p id="livesTB" style="position:absolute; right:50px; color:yellow;
    font-size:28px; font-family:Arial;">Lives: 3</p>
7   </body>
8   <script>
9       var score=0, lives=3, dogX=6, dogY=10, boneX=8, boneY=0;
10      function setLeft(id,x){document.getElementById(id).style.left=x+"px";}
11      function setTop(id,y){document.getElementById(id).style.top=y+"px";}
12      function randomNumber(low,high){return (Math.floor(low+ Math.random()*(1+high-low)));}
13      var gameTimer=window.setInterval(moveBone, 200);
14      document.onkeydown=handleKeys;
15      function handleKeys(e){
16          if(e.keyCode==37){dogX--;}
17          if(e.keyCode==39){dogX++;}
18          setLeft("dog", dogX*50);
19          setTop("dog", dogY*50);
20      }
21      function moveBone(){
22          boneY=boneY+=1;
23          setLeft("bone", boneX*50);
24          setTop("bone", boneY*50);
25          if(boneY>dogY+5){missedBone();}
26          if((dogX==boneX) && (dogY==boneY)){caughtBone();}
27      }
28      function missedBone(){
29          boneY=0;
30          boneX=randomNumber(2,16);
31          lives--;
32          document.getElementById("livesTB").innerText="Lives: "+lives;
33          if(lives==0){gameOver();}
34      }
35      function caughtBone(){
36          boneY=0;
37          boneX=randomNumber(2,16);
38          score++;
39          document.getElementById("scoreTB").innerText="Score: "+score;
40      }
41      function gameOver(){
42          alert("Game Over! You scored: "+ score);
43          location.reload();
44      }
45  </script>
46  </html>
```

GLOSSARY

ANIMATION Making objects in your program move around.

ARRAY A list of items stored as some data.

BROWSER A program used to view web pages, such as Chrome or Internet Explorer.

BUG An error in a program that stops it working properly.

DEBUG To remove bugs (or errors) from a program.

ELEMENT One of the objects making up a web page, such as a paragraph or image.

EVENT Something that happens while the program is running, such as a mouse click or key press.

FUNCTION A reusable section of code combining a number of commands.

HEXADECIMAL A system of numbers using digits from 0 to 9, then A to F.

HTML (HYPERTEXT MARKUP LANGUAGE) The language used to build web pages.

JAVASCRIPT A programming language used to make web pages interactive or to build simple games.

PIXEL A small dot on the screen. It can be used as a unit of measurement.

RANDOM NUMBER A number picked by the computer that can't be predicted.

REFRESH To load a web page again in the browser, so changes to the page can be seen.

RGB The system used to mix red, green and blue light to make any colour.

SELECTION Using commands such as IF to run different parts of a program.

STRING A type of data made of an ordered list of characters, such as 'Hello world!'.

SYNTAX Using commands, brackets and other symbols correctly and in the right order.

TAGS Special words in an HTML document surrounded by angle brackets <> defining an element.

TEXT EDITOR A program used to create and change code.

TIMER An object that runs a function after a specified delay, or at a regular interval.

VARIABLE A value used to store information in a program that can change.

BUGS & DEBUGGING

When you find your code isn't working as expected, stop and look though each line of code you have put in. Think about what you want it to do, and what it is really telling the computer to do. If you are entering one of the programs in this book, check you have not missed a line. Here are some things debugging tips:

- Check you have spelt the commands correctly.
- Check you have used the correct case (capitals or lower case).
- Check you haven't missed any quotes.
- Check you have closed tags correctly.
- If images aren't showing, check filenames have been typed accurately.
- If images aren't moving, check you have set **position:absolute**.
- Make sure you have used the correct style of brackets and other symbols.

COMMAND LIST

JAVASCRIPT COMMANDS

alert("Hello"); – shows "Hello" as a message in a pop up box.

var score=0; – defines a variable called score.

var gameTimer=window.setInterval(myFunction, 1000); – runs a function called **myFunction** every second.

clearInterval(gameTimer); – stops the timer called **gameTimer**.

function gameOver() – defines a function called **gameOver()**.

document.getElementById("dog") – selects an element on the page.

Math.random() – creates a random number between 0 and 1.

Math.round() – rounds a decimal to the nearest whole number.

location.reload(); – reloads a page to restart the JavaScript (and the game).

HTML ELEMENTS

<html>...</html> – starts and ends the HTML file.

<script>...</script> – starts and ends the script section.

<img> – defines an image, such as a photo or piece of clipart.

<p>...</p> – starts and ends a paragraph or line of text.

<body>...</body> – starts and ends the main body of the page, effectively the background of your program.

EVENTS

onclick – the mouse button has been clicked.

onmousedown – the mouse button has been pressed down (happens before click and mouse up).

onmouseup – the mouse button has been released.

onkeydown – a key has been pressed on the keyboard.

RESPECTING COPYRIGHT

Copyright means the legal ownership of something. You need to think about who owns the images or sound files you are linking to or downloading on your web page. There shouldn't be any major issues unless you try to make a page available to the public. Do check with an adult to make sure.

An alternative is to find a free to use image or sound file: search for an image or sound, then look for the **Settings** button on the website results page. Click **Advanced Search** then look for **Usage Rights**. On this menu choose **Free to use, share or modify**.

STYLE PROPERTIES

position:absolute – allows an element to be moved around by changing left and top properties.

left – sets how far across the screen an element (such as an image) is.

top – sets how far down from the top of the screen an element is.

height – sets the height of an element, such as an image (e.g. 20px means 20 pixels high).

width – sets the width of an element, such as an image.

-webkit-transition – sets how quickly an element changes its properties.

INDEX

First published in Great Britain in 2017 by Wayland

Text copyright © ICT Apps Ltd, 2017
Art and design copyright © Hodder and Stoughton Limited, 2017

All rights reserved.

Editor: Catherine Brereton
Freelance editor: Hayley Fairhead
Designer: Peter Clayman
Illustrator: Maria Cox

ISBN: 978 1 5263 0108 6
10 9 8 7 6 5 4 3 2 1

Wayland
An imprint of
Hachette Children's Group
Part of Hodder & Stoughton
Carmelite House
50 Victoria Embankment
London EC4Y 0DZ

An Hachette UK Company
www.hachette.co.uk
www.hachettechildrens.co.uk

Printed in China

The website addresses (URLs) included in this book were valid at the time of going to press. However, it is possible that contents or addresses may have changed since the publication of this book. No responsibility for any such changes can be accepted by either the author or the Publisher.

E-safety
Children will need access to the internet for most of the activities in this book. Parents or teachers should supervise this and discuss staying safe online with children.

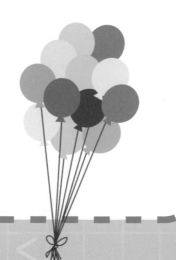